# MICHAEL
# J. FOX
## Scrapbook

D1591988

# MICHAEL J. FOX Scrapbook

## Mimi Kasbah

Ballantine Books • New York

Library of Congress Catalog Card Number: 86-92045

ISBN: 0-345-34389-1

Interior design by Michaelis/Carpelis Design Associates, Inc.
Cover design by Richard Aquan
Cover photos: Rob Lewine/Shooting Star
Manufactured in the United States of America
First Edition: June 1987
10 9 8 7 6 5 4 3 2 1

# Contents

That's right!

# Fox Facts and Figures

*Legal Name:* Michael Andrew Fox

*Birthdate:* June 9, 1961

*Birthplace:* Edmonton, Alberta, Canada

*Sign:* Gemini

*Eyes:* Blue

*Hair:* Brown

*Height:* Very close to 5′5″

*Weight:* Between 120 and 125

*Shoe Size:* 7

*Marital Status:* Single

Up a creek . . . *with* a paddle.

## Did you know . . . ?

The only nickname he'll admit to is "Mike." Aw, fess up, Michael . . . nobody makes it through life without some unusual handle.

## Did you know . . . ?

Michael once shared his digs with some oldfish, one of which was called GARP. Today he shares his life with a pit bullterrier named Burnaby and a gray cat.

*A* star from head to toe.

## Did you know . . . ?

Michael jokes that the best aspect of his height is . . . it takes no time at all to iron his pants.

## Did you know . . . ?

It seems Michael couldn't be plain old Michael Fox because another actor in the union already had bagged that moniker. He didn't like the sound of Michael A. Fox (guess why?), so he picked "J" (because of Michael J. Pollard, another star he admires).

# Fox Family Data

**A** Fox with an itch.

*Parents:* Bill and Phyllis. Bill was a career army man for 25 years; before that, he was a jockey (horses, not discs!). He now works for the Canadian Mounties. Phyllis is a secretary/payroll clerk.

*Brother:* Older brother Steven is a construction worker.

*Sisters:* Michael's two older sisters, Karen and Jackie, both have office jobs, while the youngest Fox, Kelli, is studying acting.

**M**y family is a mutual admiration society.

**I**'d love to have a couple of kids someday. And I'd raise them the way my parents raised me—with a sense of humility and respect for others.

**C**anada's home. My family's all up there, and whenever I want to feel good fast, that's where I go. It's funny because I'll sit and make all these great plans about all these wonderful places I'm going to visit, and I almost always end up going back to Vancouver.

**T**he oldest form of theatre is the dinner table. The same people every night with a new script . . .

R elaxing Alex-
style . . .
with
a tie on!

## Did you know . . . ?

Michael may be the best known comedian from
the Fox family, but when he was growing up it
was big brother Steven who got most of the
ha-has at the dinner table. In fact, Michael says
that bits of Alex's dry delivery are based on
Steven's ways of funnin'.

## Did you know . . . ?

Michael sent his parents to Europe for their
35th anniversary. One, two, three . . .
aaaawwwww.

## Did you know . . . ?

Bill and Phyllis Fox had to change their number
to "unlisted" after twenty years of blessed normalcy
when Michael's fans started to let their fingers do
the walking. Naturally, the Fox family was as polite
as possible, but when an inconsiderate few decided
to reach out and touch them in the wee hours they
gave up.

# A Few Fox Faves

*City:* Vancouver.

*Color:* Khaki.

*Food:* Chinese, burgers, and fish. "I like going out for buckets of linguini with clam sauce."

*Drink:* Diet Pepsi.

*Dessert:* Something light, like fresh fruit.

*Music:* Pretenders, U2, Joe Cocker, Elvis Costello, and Phil Collins.

*TV Shows:* "Family Ties," "Cheers," "Hill Street Blues," and "Twilight Zone."

*Movies: Diner, My Dinner with Andre, Back to the Future, Dial M for Murder,* and *Breaking Away* . . . to name a few.

*Actors:* James Cagney, Dustin Hoffman, Robert De Niro, and Kevin Bacon.

*Actresses:* Jessica Lange, Meryl Streep, and Nancy McKeon!

*Time of Day:* Night—midnight, to be exact.

*Cologne:* Something subtle, like Ralph Lauren.

A Fox with a . . . headache?

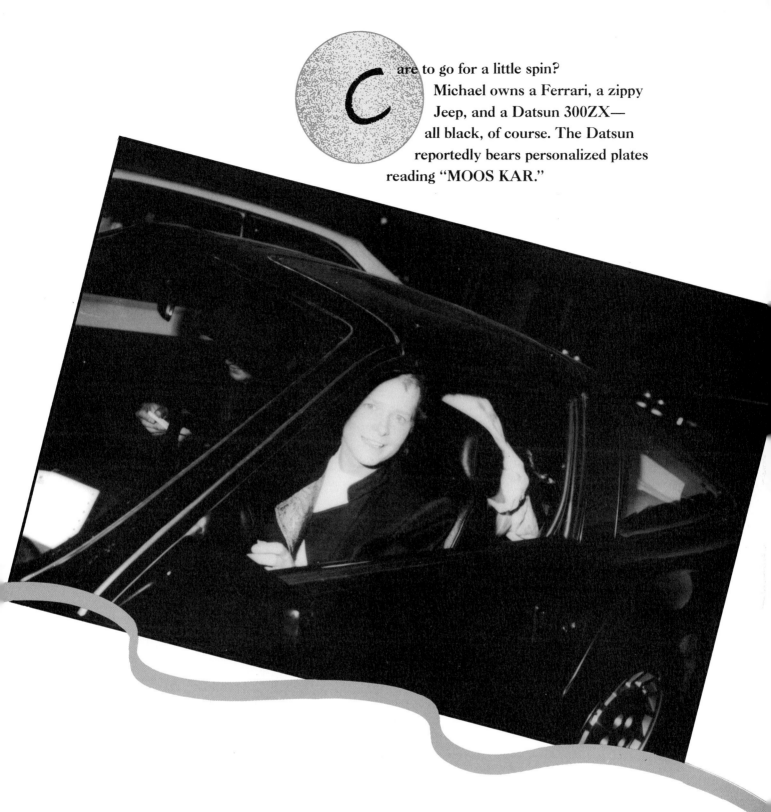

**C**are to go for a little spin? Michael owns a Ferrari, a zippy Jeep, and a Datsun 300ZX— all black, of course. The Datsun reportedly bears personalized plates reading "MOOS KAR."

## Did you know . . . ?

Michael enjoys a good scare . . . if it's on paper and in a Stephen King book.

## Did you know . . . ?

Michael was thrilled to meet Wayne Gretzky, of the Edmonton Oilers. According to most, he's the best hockey player on two skates.

## Did you know . . . ?

Michael calls Laurel Canyon (in the Hollywood Hills) his second home (besides Vancouver, natch). Included are a black-bottomed pool, a Jacuzzi, and a health spa. Be it *eva* so humble . . .

# Michael's Dreams

You may dream of Michael with the light brown hair, but what does Michael dream of? What are his ideals? Well, here's a short list:

*Dream Girl:* She's funny, intelligent, hard working, committed, and she doesn't make Michael the center of her whole universe. Most of the girls Michael dates are well groomed and attractive; full of personality and distinctive in the looks department (no paper dolls or fashion models for him).

*Dream House:* He's probably living in it right now, but luxury is not indispensable. "I would like to have a cabin in the middle of a wooded area that's only five minutes from the Paramount Studio lot where I film 'Family Ties'," he once explained.

*Dream Vacation:* Michael dreams of travelling around the world, but seldom has time to go away. So what does he do to relax at home? "Little things, like watching sports on TV, going to the fridge, opening it, looking around, not seeing anything to eat . . . closing it."

For more total relaxation, Michael loves an afternoon or weekend sport fishing. He also has a favorite hiding place. There's a certain lake near his parents' home in Vancouver that has a nice little beach for him to kick around on.

He can juggle more than starring roles.

**• • •** I have to bounce off walls.

## Did you know . . . ?

Prepare yourself. Don Johnson wants it, Bruce
Willis wants it, Michael J. Fox wants it. What
is it, Cybill Shepherd? Naaah, it's a second career
in the music biz. Michael is interested in putting
together a band and hitting the road during
any future breaks, even if he has to rehearse
around his job.

## Did you know . . . ?

If he hadn't chosen acting,
Michael might have been
an artist.

A new look for Michael.

Before I started acting, I wanted
to be a rock 'n' roller. I also used
to write a lot of short stories. I
wrote about everything, but I especially
loved writing mysteries.

# Canada . . . O Canada: A Star Is Born

When Michael was born on June 9th, 1961, he wasn't the big cheese he is today, but the future star of film and small screen was a featured member of the Fox clan's own edition of "Family Ties."

Big Daddy Bill moved the Fox family all over creation (but within the Canadian borders) for the first ten years of Michael's existence, following the whims and wisdom of the Canadian Armed Forces. Then Bill and his wife, Phyllis, landed in Vancouver, and there they stayed.

Michael grew up in a happy home with an older brother and three sisters, so it's easy to see why he gets along with other people so well! However, this totally active guy was also a totally active kid, and he found plenty of time between family fun and games to develop his own interests.

If you think that Michael is hard to keep up with now, check out his interests when he was growing up: writing and drawing and reading were his indoors sports, swimming and racquetball and hockey were his outdoor sports. Even after he discovered acting and started turning his energy toward it, Michael kept up with most of his other activities. But acting gave his life a little special something; "I was always kind of a hyper kid . . . acting gave me a creative outlet for all my energy."

Michael was also a real firebrand in school; he hurdled around the ice with the hockey team, and fronted a rock 'n' roll band called Halex (they got the name from a brand of ping-pong ball) in his spare time. Michael was once the president of the drama club, but rumor has it that he actually failed his high school drama class!

These days, Michael doesn't have as much time as he'd like for his various hobbies and passions; he's channeled all of his vigor into his career. Michael comments, "I don't know if I'd call myself hyper . . . I'm just very focused."

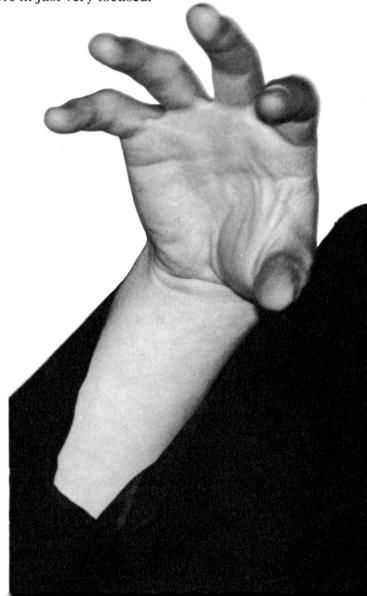

*M*y mother used to worry because I was always small for my age and I acted so crazy at times! But my grand mother always said, 'Don't worry, he'll get through it, and then he'll be famous someday. . . . I just wish she had lived long enough to see me now.

*T*his teen wolf sports *two* earrings.

**I** try not to worry too much about my future. I don't like to plan things out in advance. I'd rather live my life sort of spur-of-the-moment.

PROPERTY

## *Did you know . . . ?*

Our man of steel works out with trendy fitness guru Jake (just call him "Body by . . .") three times a week. "I was getting scared," confesses Michael. "I was seeing my childhood friends getting older, still boasting about how much they could eat, and some of them getting huge. I was thinking, You know, you've got to get on top of this thing sometime between the age of 25 or 30, or it's all over for you."

# Into the Lion's Den (In Which the Quick Fox Outdistances All Lazy Dogs)

If it all goes tomorrow, I'll be fishing.

Michael's entrance into the big bad world of showbiz sort of snuck up on him. His junior high drama teacher pointed him towards an audition at the CBC (Canadian Broadcasting Company) for a regional TV series called "Leo And Me." Michael says he went after the part on a dare, because the call was for a lively and clever 10-year-old—and he'd already hit the ripe age of 15! ". . . Being 15 years old, I figured I'd be the brightest 10-year-old kid they'd ever seen," he jokes now. "At the time I was 3'11″ and weighed 85 pounds. After I auditioned they thought I was a genius."

When the producers found out that their brilliant discovery was a member in good standing of the teen set, they decided to hire him anyhow. What they didn't anticipate in Michael's future was the sudden onslaught of hormones that changed his voice and height. Michael's voice got pretty low (especially for a supposed 10 year old) and he grew three inches within a mere six episodes. Nevertheless, Michael remained on the show for two seasons—sporting a real "Prince Valiant" style hairdo!

Once he was bitten by the acting bug, Michael found it difficult to deny, particularly after he experienced live theatre. One of the biggest influences on him was a play he performed in called *The Shadow Box*. "It was at that time that I started to understand what a noble profession theater is. And that's when I started to think of myself as an actor."

17

# The Long, Lean and Loathsome Years

Small and sexy!

Michael ended up leaving school to pursue his dream. He's never really regretted his decision, but he doesn't recommend it, either. "I don't want to give the impression that dropping out of school is the thing to do. . . . It just happened to work for me." It worked for him alright . . . eventually.

When Michael turned 18, he struck out for the fabulous, glamorous life in swinging Hollywood, U.S.A. His parents were very supportive; they gave him three thousand dollars and Bill drove him down to California. The first night, they stayed in a hotel. The next day, Michael secured an apartment and went out to conquer the world.

When asked to assess this fearless move, Michael admits that he was a bit foolhardy at the time. He'd grown up in a close, tightknit family, and he had no idea how to take care of himself. Consequently, when the jobs didn't come in fast and furious, Michael didn't know how to cope. He spent money without regard for his future and got into debt. He ended up in a rather dreary basement apartment eating beans and macaroni. Things got pretty bad. "I had a sectional sofa and I sold it, section by section, as things got worse and worse... I like the idea of these sections going around Hollywood from actor to actor."

Michael also had to learn how to deal

18

**I** didn't get into acting because I thought it was easy.

with the heavy competition as well as the blasé attitude of the people in the industry, and he took rejection very personally.

One of his biggest disappointments also taught him a very important lesson. Michael heard that Robert Redford was casting for a film called "Ordinary People," and Michael thought the part of the son sounded tailor made for him. Financially he was rather desperate at the time, so he did some extra homework. Bagging a contraband script was difficult, but he managed to do it and spent days and nights poring over his lines. Michael became really obsessed with the role and thought of nothing else.

Unfortunately, Michael's appointment with Redford was set for very early in the morning. Michael had spent the previous night filming instead of resting . . . but that wasn't the big problem. The big problem was one of chemistry. Michael claims that Redford hated him the moment he laid eyes on him.

The woman in charge of casting liked Michael and tried to stick up for him. She told Mr. Redford to have a bit of pity because of Michael's exhaustion, but the boss wasn't impressed. He replied that all Hollywooders keep crazy hours. Then, according to Michael, he spent the rest of the interview flossing his teeth.

Michael didn't get the part. Tim Hutton did, and *he* won an Oscar for it. But these days, Michael considers it water under the bridge—and he never again let himself wrap up so much hope in a prospective part.

*I*'m more levelheaded now . . . If I'd won the lead role of *Back To The Future* six years ago . . . I think I would have been placing bids to buy small islands by now.

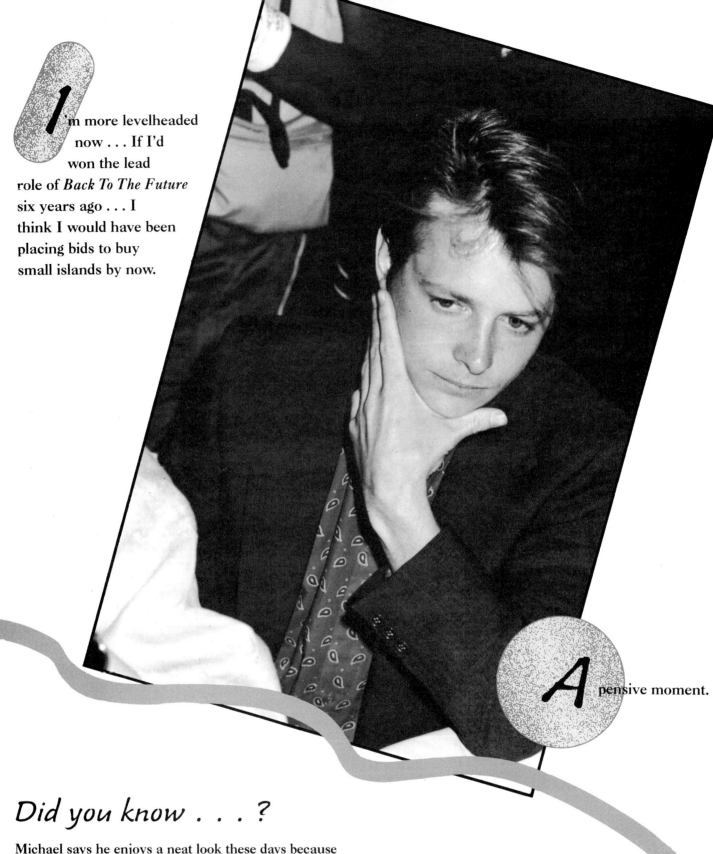

*A* pensive moment.

## Did you know . . . ?

Michael says he enjoys a neat look these days because he had to look scruffy for all those years while he was spending his money on important things, like macaroni and cheese.

## Did you know . . . ?

Ever wonder who got Michael's couch? It was Lance Guest, of the film *The Last Starfighter*.

# Michael's Early Road to Stardom

"Leo and Me," a Canadian TV series, featured a 15-year-old Michael as 10-year-old Jamie Romano.

*The Shadow Box* was Michael's first exploration of live theatre.

Michael filmed *Letters from Frank* (1979) with the legendary Art Carney and Maureen Stapleton. This movie chronicled the sad story of a guy with a job at a newspaper who is forced to retire when his workload is taken over by a computer.

*Class of 1984* (1982) was a high-school-horror-punks-on-the-rampage howler starring Tim Van Patten as leading rotten apple. Other stars included Perry King and Roddy McDowall.

"Palmerstown" was a Norman Lear series on CBS which also starred Lori Lethin. When Norman Lear was asked why he cast M.J.F. in "Palmerstown" he replied, "I saw him, heard him, loved him. He was wonderful in a very small role. I didn't give him too much opportunity, but Michael made everything he could of it."

*Midnight Madness* (1980) was not a very good film at all by most people's reckoning, but distinctive because it was the first Disney film to be rated PG. The story line centered on a batch of college students and their nightlong scavenger hunt.

*High School U.S.A.* (1983) was a made-for-television movie starring

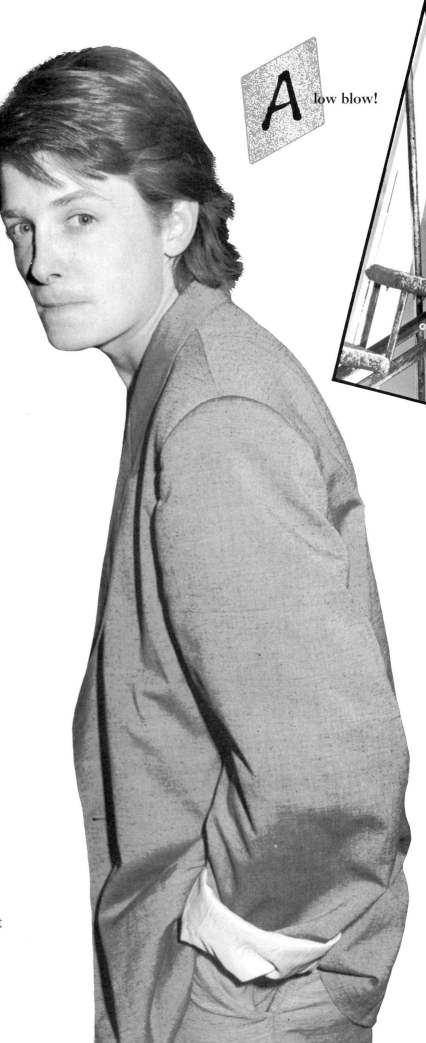

A low blow!

Michael and Nancy McKeon. Michael played J.J. Manners. One of the other stars was one Crispin Glover, who later popped up as Marty McFly's dad in *Back to the Future*. This movie also starred some notables from the early years of teens on TV, such as Bob Denver (Maynard G. Krebs), Dwayne Hickman (Dobie Gillis), Tony Dow (Wally Cleaver), and Elinor Donahue (of "Father Knows Best").

*Poison Ivy* (1985), another made-for-TV movie, was a "camp" comedy which starred Michael, Nancy McKeon, Caren Kaye, and Robert Klein. Michael played the counselor/romeo to the hilt, pursuing Nancy with an insatiable urge to merge. Comedian Klein, as the nitwit camp director, was his admirable foil.

"I know it sounds real cornball, but I'm genuinely grateful for the things I've been able to do and the support I've had from people."

# Television Bit Parts

Michael made guest appearances on great shows such as "Lou Grant," "Trapper John M.D.," "The Love Boat," and "Family" (which also starred Meredith Baxter Birney!).

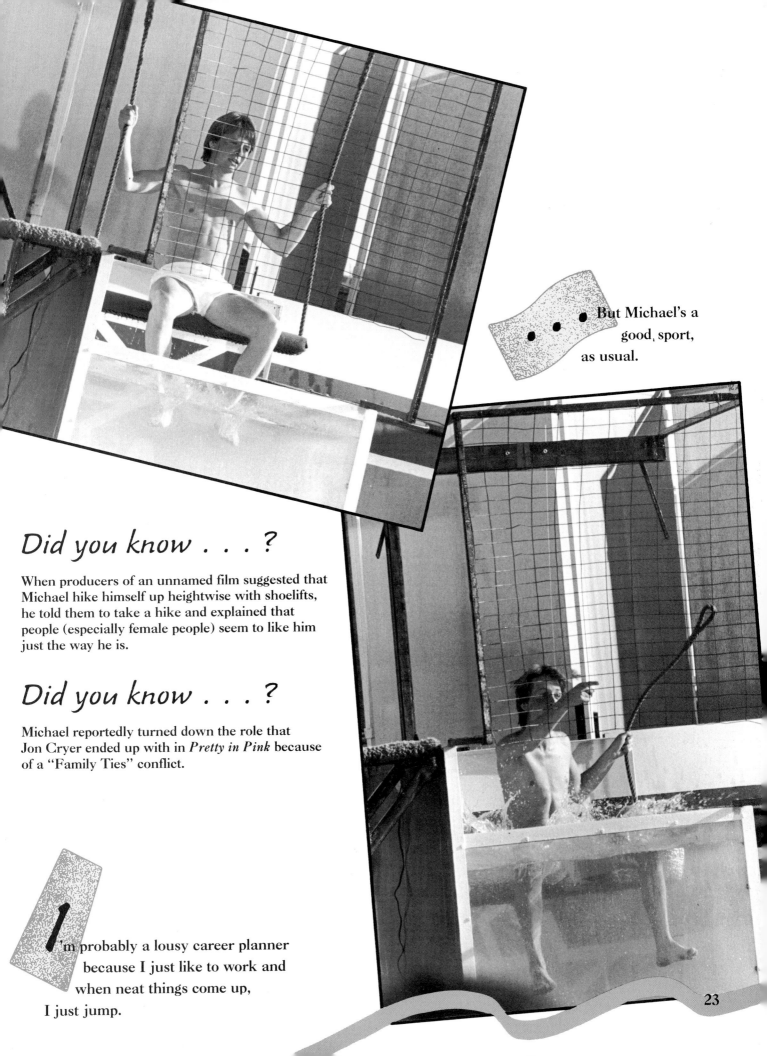

But Michael's a good, sport, as usual.

## Did you know . . . ?

When producers of an unnamed film suggested that Michael hike himself up heightwise with shoelifts, he told them to take a hike and explained that people (especially female people) seem to like him just the way he is.

## Did you know . . . ?

Michael reportedly turned down the role that Jon Cryer ended up with in *Pretty in Pink* because of a "Family Ties" conflict.

'm probably a lousy career planner because I just like to work and when neat things come up, I just jump.

# Family Ties: Jacket and Tie Required

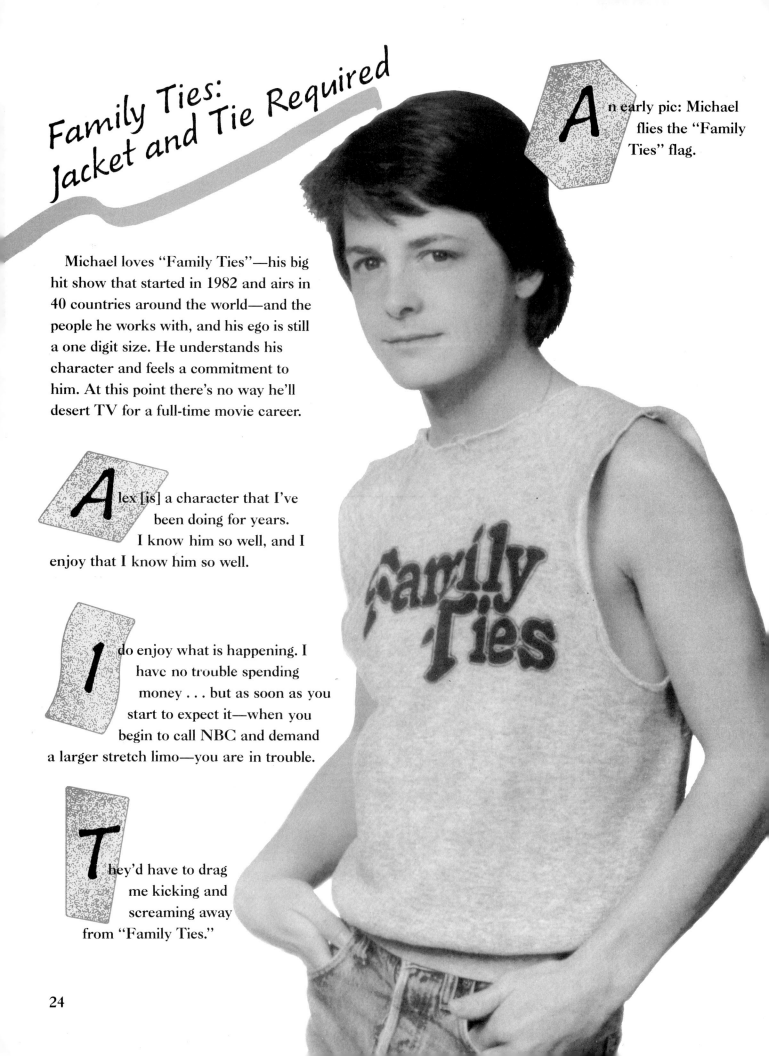

An early pic: Michael flies the "Family Ties" flag.

Michael loves "Family Ties"—his big hit show that started in 1982 and airs in 40 countries around the world—and the people he works with, and his ego is still a one digit size. He understands his character and feels a commitment to him. At this point there's no way he'll desert TV for a full-time movie career.

Alex [is] a character that I've been doing for years. I know him so well, and I enjoy that I know him so well.

I do enjoy what is happening. I have no trouble spending money . . . but as soon as you start to expect it—when you begin to call NBC and demand a larger stretch limo—you are in trouble.

They'd have to drag me kicking and screaming away from "Family Ties."

24

On the set of "Family Ties."

Michael with his "little brother," Brian Bonsall.

Every medium—movies, TV, stage—is valid. . . . I don't think that television is something I want to break away from, and I don't see it as a stepping stone to something 'bigger.' Being on television is my job and I care about it. . . . Just because it's on videotape instead of film doesn't make it any less important.

**W**henever Alex is feeling depressed . . . he'll walk around in jeans or a T-shirt. But when he's feeling really great about himself, he'll have the tie on—even when he's sitting around watching TV.

**M**ichael was really proud of his Emmy, which he received in 1986 for his work on "Family Ties."

**T**he award winner! Michael posing with his hefty plaque at the 26th International Broadcasting Awards at the Century Plaza Hotel in L.A. after he was named Man of the Year in Broadcasting.

26th ANNUAL INTERNATIONAL BROADCASTING AWARDS

MAN of the YEAR IN BROADCASTING

1985

MICHAEL J. FOX

Star Of
NBC - Paramount Series

"FAMILY TIES"

Presented By

HOLLYWOOD RADIO
and TELEVISION SOCIETY

March 18, 1986
Century Plaza Hotel
Los Angeles

With Meredith Baxter Birney and Michael Gross at a 1983 press conference.

# Family Ties Vacation

In 1985, Alex and Mallory et al. travelled to the *very* unsunny climes of Great Britain for a closer look at that famous stiff upper lip. Michael J. was delighted by the friendly people he met . . . and totally revolted by the disgusting food that they ate! It was a good time to go on a bread and water diet, bypassing the eels and toast covered in yeast paste.

On a lighter note, Michael discovered a real Canadian-style pub right in the middle of Covent Garden. He spent most of his time there, talking hockey with other transplants from the Great White North. Michael enjoyed it so much that he became quite homesick; and when filming ended, he made a stop in Vancouver on his way to L.A.

Brother" and "sister" at a Special Olympics benefit.

## Did you know . . . ?

Michael can skate and play the guitar and do many
other things, but he's always had a problem tying knots
in his neckties (don't tell Alex!).

## Did you know . . . ?

Because "Alex P. Keaton" is Mr. Straight-Arrow
Republican, the Committee for the Reelection of Ronald
Reagan actually approached Michael to be a spokesman,
but he declined politely, reminding them that he's not
even American born and doesn't feel right getting
involved in U.S. politics. Come on, you guys—didn't
your mom ever tell you not to believe everything you
see on TV?

With most of the Keaton family at a
celebration of their 100th
show. Left to right: Meredith
Baxter Birney, Brian Bonsall,
Michael Gross, Justine Bateman, and some
guy who's always having his picture
taken with famous people.

**T**he Man of the Year celebrates.

**A** youthful Fox attends Justine Bateman's "Sweet 16" birthday party in Beverly Hills.

## Did you know . . . ?

It is rumored that Michael makes a million just for re-signing his contract for "Family Ties." On top of that he may rake in over $80,000 per episode. Whatta lotta bananas!

## Did you know . . . ?

Believe it or not, the producers of "Family Ties" almost dropped Michael during his first season as Alex P. Keaton. Luckily they reconsidered!

29

**A**rriving at the Grammy Awards at the Shrine Auditorium in L.A.

**C**lose enough to touch . . .

I am not working. This is what I do. I'm an actor. I'm having a blast.

M ichael with his mean machine.

M ichael with his moose collection.

**S**peaking out for Amnesty International.

**M**ichael in a bind.

*W*haddya mean,
hold the mayo?

H e can be moody and intense.

*I'*d much rather spend my time making people laugh than chasing lots of girls all over the place.

*A*cting helps me get away from the pressures of just being "me." I can be another character for a while, and that's a lot of fun.

**S**howing off some fancy footwear.

**T**he old soft shoe.

**W**hat, me worry?

He can be as serious
as Alex.

## Hits and Misses on the Big Screen

# Teen Wolf

*Teen Wolf* starred Michael as an adolescent boy with the usual adolescent problems—plus one whompin' big unusual problem. "Scott Howard" discovers his heredity one day under duress: he's a werewolf! By the end of the picture, Scott learns quite a lot about himself.

Michael had five weeks off from "Family Ties" during which he filmed this comedy. His wolf makeup took four hours to put on and one hour to take off *every day*, so almost six solid days were spent fiddling with fang teeth and hairy lips. Michael picked the script out of the many submitted to him because he felt it wasn't a 'teensploitation' flick, but in retrospect he's not too keen on the film or his performance. However, there are no regrets on Michael's part. As usual, he can take it lightly.

## Did you know . . . ?

Officially, in 1986 Michael had only four days off.

Michael will sign just about anything for his fans.

# Back to the Future

*Back to the Future* needs no introduction to most of the movie-going population. In this box-office smash Michael starred as "Marty McFly," a boy who travels into the past and has an exciting encounter with his parents-to-be.

When Michael heard about this Steven Spielberg film he considered trying out, but his work with "Family Ties" conflicted and he decided to pass. Eric Stolz (*Mask*) was cast at first, but he lasted only a few weeks for reasons unknown (probably creative differences). Gary Goldberg, one of the "Family Ties" producers, is a friend of Spielberg's. He suggested Michael, on the condition that his part be filmed at night, after his regular job. Michael got the script on Wednesday and went to work the following Monday. Things began to get very crazy. "Nine A.M. to six P.M. would be spent at 'Family Ties'; Six P.M. to three A.M. would be spent at Universal . . . after which a driver would take me and literally deposit me on my bed," Michael told *USA Today*.

*A*s long as I know where my priorities are, as long as I bust my butt to do good work . . . and realize what's important, that's going to reflect in some way.

*E*ven I'm surprised at the big leap my career has taken in the last few years. But I realize that it might not last forever. That's why I'm working so hard to stay in the public eye. He means by making movies, not by going to parties.)

"Seven weeks of this made me feel very surrealistic—I reasoned that Michael J. Fox was only a lifeless form sleeping between jobs." Later he admitted that towards the end of "Family Ties" filming, ". . . my brain seriously started to turn to cheese, but I just kept going."

Michael was driven by pure determination because he knew that even if the movie did not turn out to be a huge success, it was a great opportunity. He shored up his determination with doses of vitamins (he was willing to try anything!). Everybody admired his unflagging energy, so Michael felt even more inspired to keep on a good face. He'd wait until he got home to collapse. Then he'd sleep in sweat pants and a T-shirt so he could jump out of bed and into the world.

One of the best parts in the film is Marty McFly's rendition of "Johnny B. Goode" with a group called the Starlighters. It was something that Michael just happened to be prepared for. Three months before, he'd bought a Fender guitar and started practicing. Michael actually got good enough to play some guitar in the movie, but what you hear on the soundtrack album is the work of a studio player. Still, Michael was thrilled when Marty McFly and the Starlighters actually got onto the billboard charts with "Johnny B. Goode."

Michael also appeared in a video with Huey Lewis and the News for "The Power of Love," a hit from the soundtrack. Huey appeared in the film in a cameo as the high school teacher who says that the Starlighters are "too loud." He said that Michael was the best fake guitar player he'd ever seen!

## Did you know . . . ?

When Michael was switching between *Back to the Future* and "Family Ties" he had what he called collapsible hair. He could wear it up or down, with a little help from the other kind of mousse.

## Did you know . . . ?

Figure this out: The California Raisin Advisory Board (did you even know there was such an animal?) paid the producers of *Back to the Future* big bucks to have Mr. Marty McFly chew a few during his futuristic adventure. The scene was cut—and the only raisin to be seen in the flick was in total 2D (as in 2 dumb) as an advertisement barely visible on a vagrant-covered bench. The Raisin Bunch decided that they wanted their $50,000 back, pronto.

*I* just do the best I can.

# Light of Day

*Light Of Day* is a significant film for Michael J. Fox, for it marks his debut as a dramatic actor. Everyone who is familiar with Michael's work knows and enjoys his versatility in the field of comedy, but until *Light Of Day*, most of us hadn't gotten a chance to see much of his "serious" side.

Joan Jett, rock 'n' roll femme extraordinaire, plays Michael's older sis. Veterans Gena Rowlands and Jason Miller are their parents. Michael plays 22-year-old Joe Resnick, a factory worker whose hardest jobs are keeping his family together and resolving his conflicts with his sister as they try to make their way in a band.

During the movie, you see a very unfamiliar Michael, one who smokes and drinks and gets into trouble. Though these surface traits aren't necessarily a part of Michael's life, he feels quite close to Joe Resnick and his dilemmas.

The original title of *Light Of Day* was *Born in the U.S.A.*, which probably sounds extremely familiar. "The Boss" happens to be a friend of Paul Schrader (the project's mastermind), and when Springsteen read the script it inspired him to pen the big hit tune. Later, the movie's title was changed . . . but a platinum reminder will always be with us!

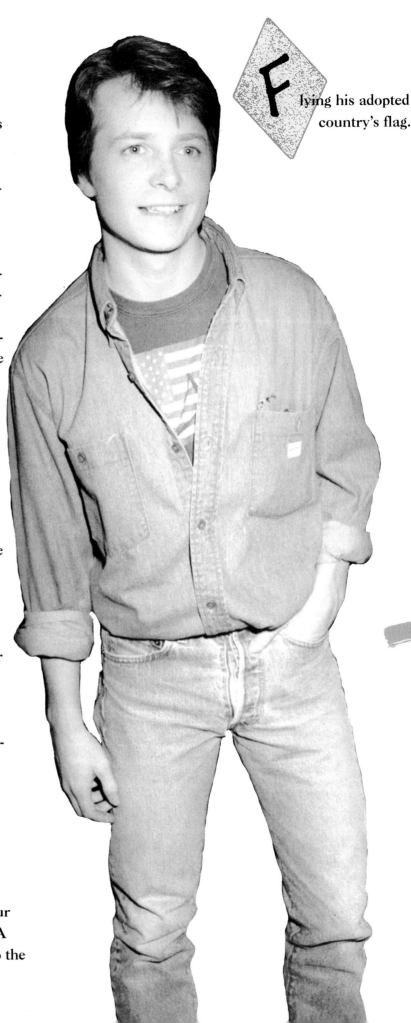

**F**lying his adopted country's flag.

**I** just wanted to do something *real*, where if you blow your nose you blow your nose. A movie where people went to the bathroom.

**M**ichael scores for the *Light of Day* team!

## Did you know . . . ?

Michael actually does smoke, but you'll never see him doing it in public. Advisors pointed out that it might set a bad example, and he agreed.

## Did you know . . . ?

Michael loves his fans, but during *Light of Day* filming so many gathered around a building the cast and crew were using for interior shots that he hired a double to help him get in and out in one piece. Later the poor guy, who was practically stampeded, said, "I never want to be that famous. It scared me to death!"

## Did you know . . . ?

Jett on Fox: "You've got to give the guy credit. He can really play."

## Did you know . . . ?

Though he protested he'd never record ("Recording is something I'll never do because I don't sing very well"), Michael has finally broken into vinyl. You'll hear him warbling on the *Light of Day* title track.

# The Secret of My Success

In this romantic comedy, Michael plays a sharp young man from Kansas named Brantley Foster who travels East to New York City with the intention of getting rich and famous as quickly as possible. He goes to his uncle, who's a big wheel in the business world, and asks for a job. Brantley's uncle isn't at all interested in helping out, but a chance encounter with a high-powered board member pans out into gainful employment.

While working in the accounting department, Brantley meets his uncle's wife. She gets a yen for him, makes a big play, and he eventually gives in (who ever said accounting is dull?). Things get even more complicated when he ends up as his uncle's assistant and meets a gorgeous woman (Helen Slater) who turns out to be his uncle's mistress. Naturally they fall in love during the ensuing entanglements and there's a happy (and surprising) ending for all.

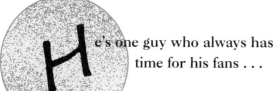 He's one guy who always has time for his fans . . .

## Did you know . . . ?

When a bodyguard on the location of *The Secret of My Success* told some loitering Fox fans to vacate the area, Michael practically blew a fuse. "Don't ever talk to my fans that way!" he shouted. "If it weren't for them, I wouldn't be where I am today!" He spent the next twenty minutes signing whatever was put in front of him.

At one point they wrote jokes about Alex's height, but the audience didn't laugh . . . Alex, like myself, doesn't really know he's short, so it's not funny.

# Future Projects

You'll be seeing quite a lot of Michael in the years to come because this dynamo has no intention of slowing down. Scheduled for completion ASAP (as soon as possible) is the untitled sequel to *Back To The Future*. Michael is also interested in doing a comedy for Walt Disney studios about the first male student to attend Vassar.

But Michael's most important project may be a movie about young Jimmy Cagney, which Cagney requested Michael star in. Michael was appearing on a TV talk show when his idol called personally to ask him to take the part, and Michael was moved to tears.

You also may be seeing Michael in another important role in *The Kirk Crocker Story*, the sad tale of a young man with radiation poisoning.

**M**ichael sports the native dress of his country . . . a lumberjack shirt!

**I**'m afraid someone will take it all away if I'm a jerk about it. I think one day they'll figure out I'm this ugly little runt from Canada with too many hockey scars on his body and the whole thing will go out the window.

# Michael's People

Michael claims that he's one man who isn't much of a social animal, but the pictures seem to tell a different story. Actually, Michael really does prefer to curl up at home with some hot guitar licks or a good video cassette, but in the course of promoting his movies—*and* the various charities he supports, *and* big events like the Amnesty International Concert and the celebration for the Statue of Liberty— Michael gets around with some very glittering company. This hardworking guy can party with the best of 'em!

**M**ichael arrives at the South Street Seaport in New York City (escorted by two Canadian Mounted Police, minus mounts) at the Canadian tribute to the Statue of Liberty. A twenty-one moose call salute?

**M**ichael and Whoopi Goldberg at the Academy Awards.

**M**y friends back home assume that because I'm out here in Hollywood with a successful TV series and a hit movie under my belt, all I do is party! They think I go to nightclubs every night, but that's not true at all—I'm usually too tired. So when I go home for a visit, my buddies practically kill me by taking me to one nightclub after another, until I'm so wiped out that I fall back on my mother's couch and sleep for about three days.

**I** look for friends who don't make a big deal over what I do for a living. Acting is just my job. Being an actor doesn't make me better than anyone else.

**M**ichael and Nancy McKeon make the scene at the Shrine Auditorium in L.A. at opening night festivities for the American Ballet Theatre.

**S**omeone stop this crazy bus—
we wanna get off!
A wacky moment with
Michael and his copresenter Rebecca
De Mornay at the 58th annual Academy
Awards.

**A**t the People's Choice Awards, Appolonia
tells Michael the secret of *her*
success . . .

## Did you know . . . ?

Michael spends a lot of time doing charity work and playing the good samaritan, but he prefers to keep it quiet. He's accepted such challenges as the national chairmanship of public awareness for the Spina Bifida Association.

**R**ob Lowe and Michael show their fists of fury at the Hagler-Mugabi match at Caesar's Palace, Las Vegas.

**A**t a party in New York City, explaining to Rolling Stone Ron Wood the results of putting one and one together.

**M**ichael with Howie Mandel and his new friend, A. Emmy. Proud Michael let his parents take the special statue up to Canada for a while.

**W**ith Mark Harmon at the "Battle of the Network Stars."

**A** new look? No, just protective gear for the "Battle of the Network Stars" (those network stars fight dirty) at Pepperdine University in Malibu.

**M** ichael plays the fall guy at the "Battle of the Network Stars."

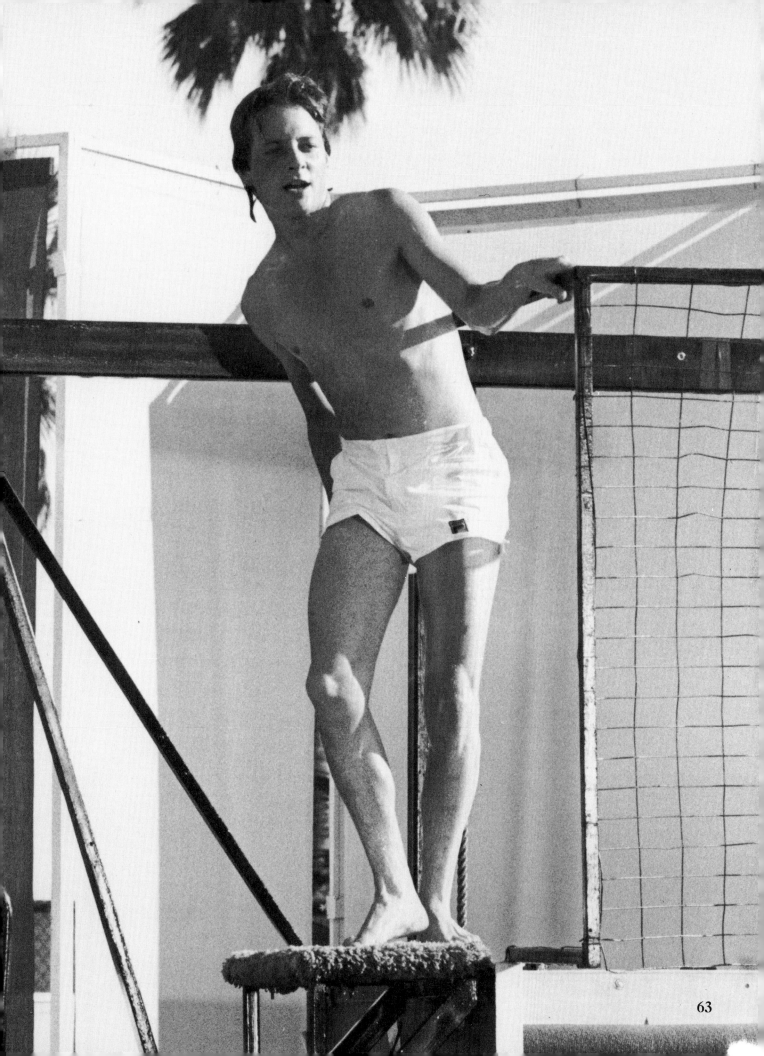

**P**al Julian Lennon tells Michael the history of his hat. Michael is good friends with pop star Julian and even made a brief appearance in one of his videos. The two met at an L.A. film premiere and became fast buddies.

**W**ith Carly Simon at New York's Hard Rock Cafe.

# Did you know . . . ?

Michael does read his fan mail whenever he gets a chance, but since he gets over 21,000 letters a week (more than anyone else on TV) he needs quite a lot of help answering your cards and letters.

Even though Michael gets all that fan mail, he won't let NBC start an official fan club for him. Michael states that he doesn't want to be idolized because "I'm just an actor." Instead, he makes sure that he's available for tons of interviews and photo sessions.

Clowning around with Molly Ringwald at the premiere of Julian Lennon's video.

**P**icking up a few tips from Sugar Ray Leonard

**H**obknobbing with Burt Reynolds.

**M**ustachioed Michael and his manager leave fashionable Spago's restaurant in California.

**M**ichael with Tracy Pollen (Alex's former "Family Ties" sweetheart, "Ellen") at the 43rd annual Golden Globe Awards held at the super-glamorous Beverly Hilton Hotel. Tracy actually dates handsome Kevin Bacon.

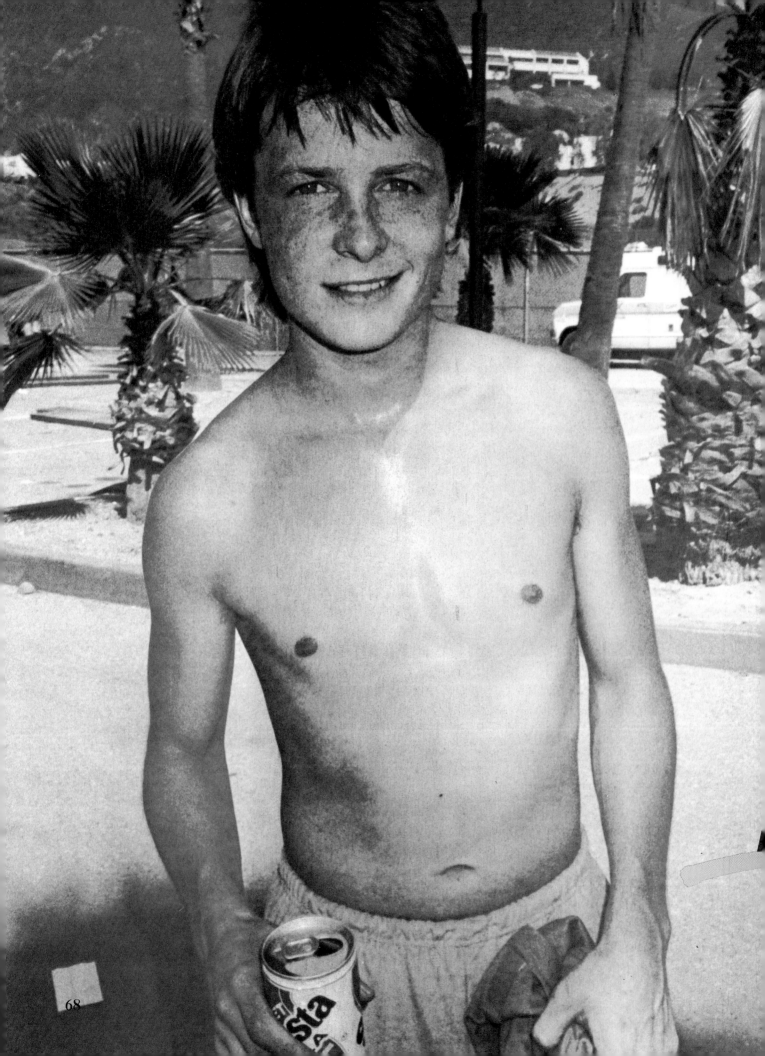

**W**hat the . . . ? A temporarily
furry Fox in 1986.

**A** cool break with a hot Fox.

# Foxy Fox

**W**hen I was in high school, I didn't date very much because I was so short—I just wasn't very confident in myself. Now I think I've got a lot more going for me, but I'm still shy.

**I**f you're a Libra, Aquarius, Leo, or Aries, you might be this Gemini guy's type!

**T**he way my schedule has been, I'm not seeing a lot of anybody. I've hardly even seen myself!

**P**ainting the town with Kari Michaelson of ("Gimme a Break") in 1983.

**I** know it may be hard to believe, but I'm quite shy around girls. Even if I like a girl a lot, it usually takes me months to ask her out. I guess you could say I'm slightly bashful.

Michael met ex-steady Nancy McKeon when they costarred in *High School U.S.A.* The dynamic duo also filmed *Poison Ivy* together before Michael moved on. Remember, Geminis need to be constantly occupied and they love to meet new people.

When Michael parted from date-mate Nancy he was immediately bombarded with hundreds of marriage proposals from all over the country. However, Michael has no problem finding companionship.

In one of those sometimes-life-imitates-art occurrences, Michael and Helen Slater dated for a while during the filming of *The Secret of My Success*, and their romance got more media attention than the movie itself. Michael wasn't really interested in dating anyone at that point; he had just broken up with Nancy McKeon and wanted to play the field a bit. Then infatuation struck, and he and Helen spent their spare time together, hitting the nightspots and dayspots of New York City. They even went on a double date with Julian Lennon and his girlfriend.

On Michael's 25th Birthday he flew Bill and Phyllis to NYC. Michael, his parents and Helen went to see the play *Loot* and things seemed to be getting serious. A couple of weeks later, however, Michael decided that he needed to concentrate on his work more so he and Helen split.

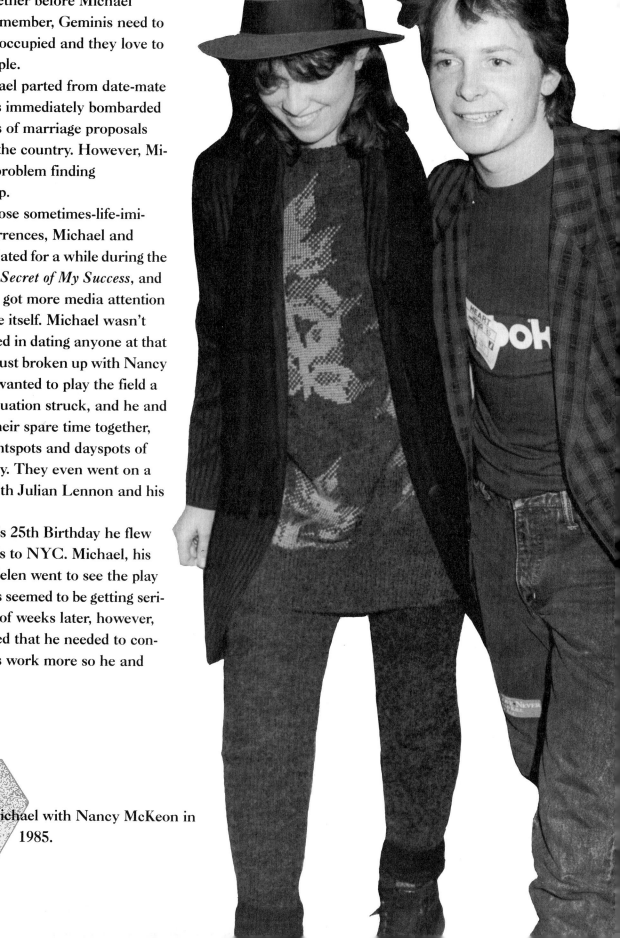

Michael with Nancy McKeon in 1985.

**I** can just feel it when a friendship is right.

**M**ichael shares a quiet moment with Helen Slater on the set of *The Secret of My Success*.

**M**ichael and Jennifer Gray (you saw her in *Ferris Bueller's Day Off*) catch the spotlight at the premiere of *Pretty in Pink* at Mann's Chinese Theatre in Hollywood.

F oxy, foxy.

**I**f a girl can sit for an hour and a half in a cold ice rink and watch me play hockey, it's usually a good sign, because that's something I enjoy a lot.

**W**hen I was 15, I thought I would have kids when I was 30. Now that I'm 24, I think 35 would be a good idea.

**I** never tried to date a girl because she is 5′1″. I wouldn't think twice if she was 5′8″.

*T*om Cruise isn't the only one who can look cool with a pair of Ray-Bans. (Hey, Michael, they're supposed to go on your *face*!)

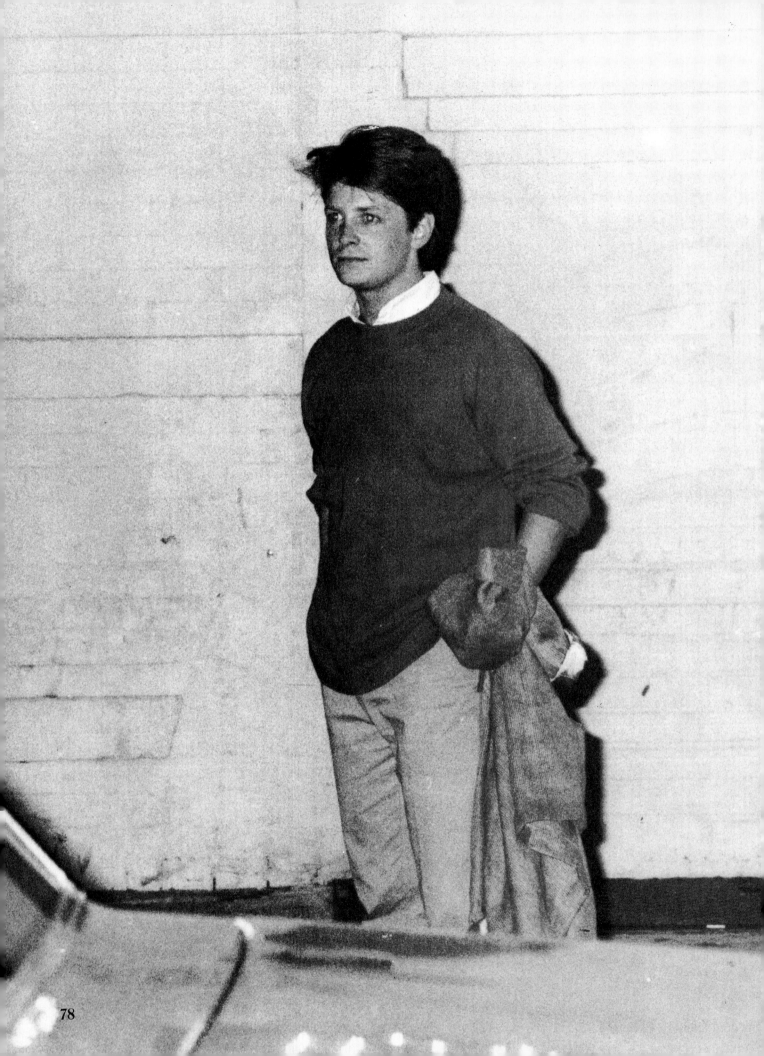

About the Author

Mimi Kasbah likes to travel incognito, watch *Dobie Gillis* reruns, and write haiku with crayons. This is her second book.

# Photo Credits